100 FIRST WORDS
Dutch Edition
Reading 3rd Grade
Children's Reading & Writing Books

Do you want
to learn some
common Dutch
words?

Let's get started!

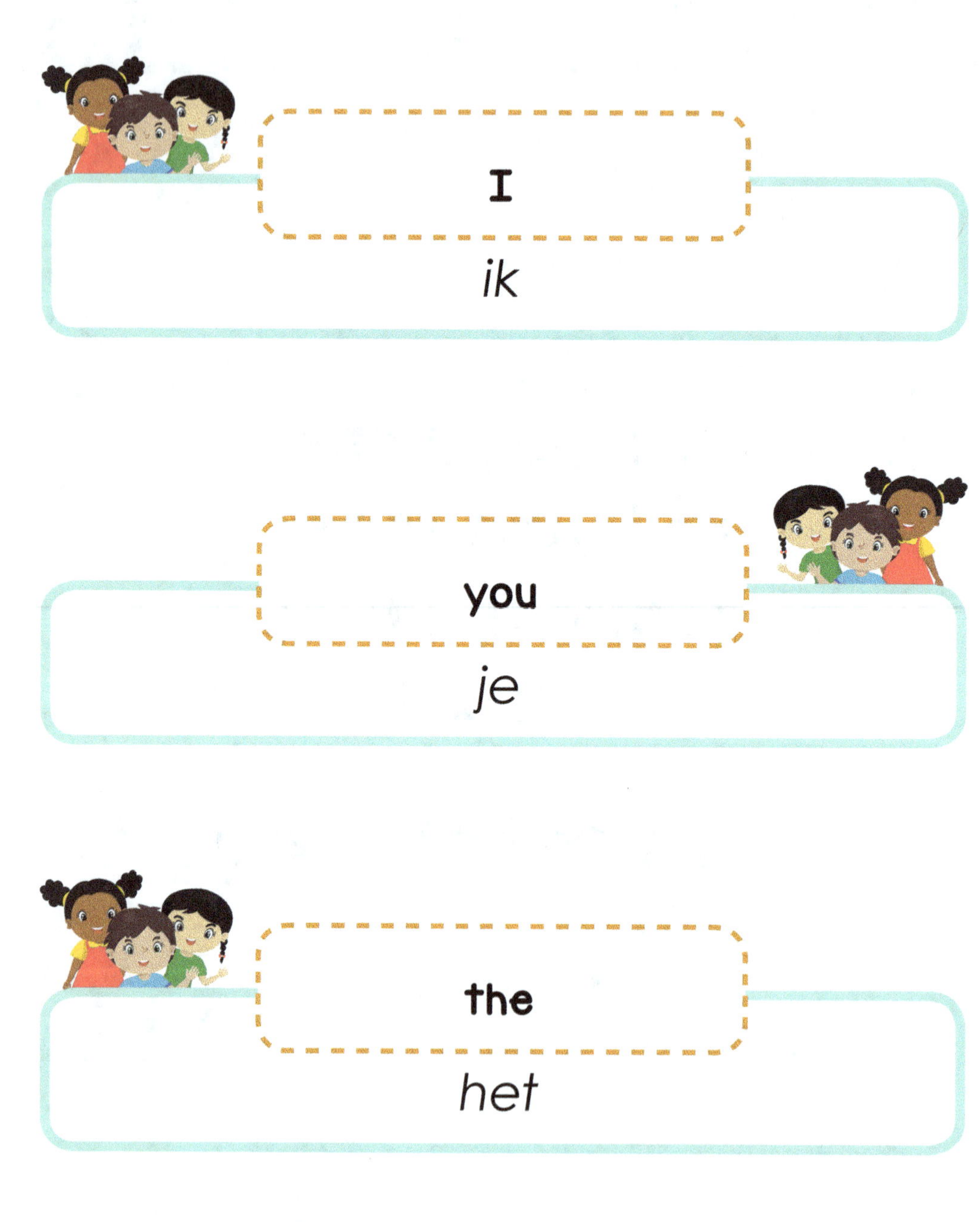

I
ik

you
je

the
het

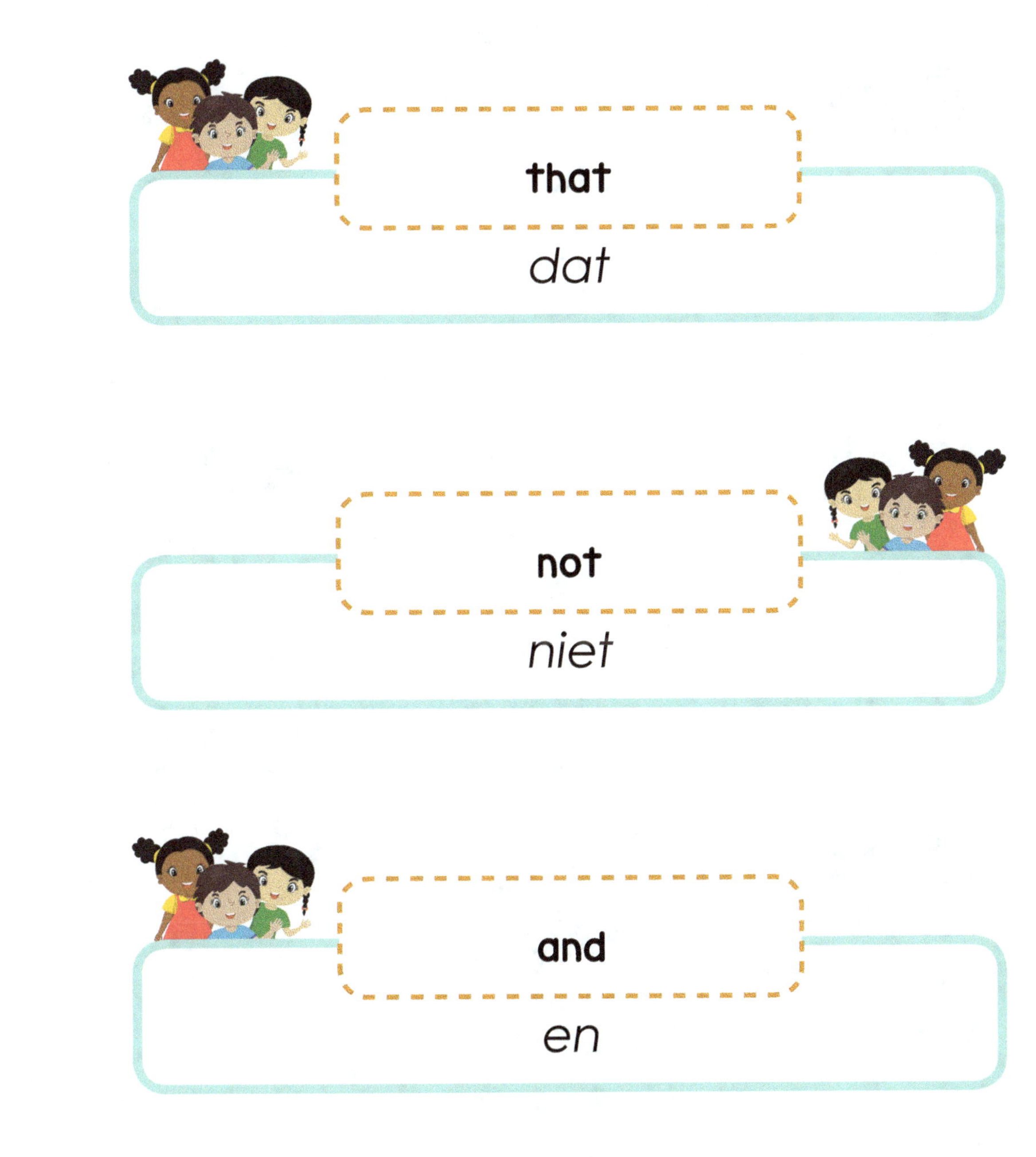
that
dat
not
niet
and
en

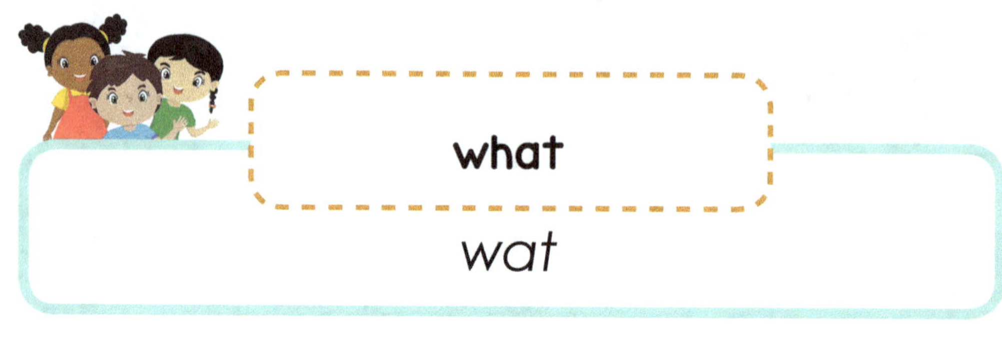

what
wat

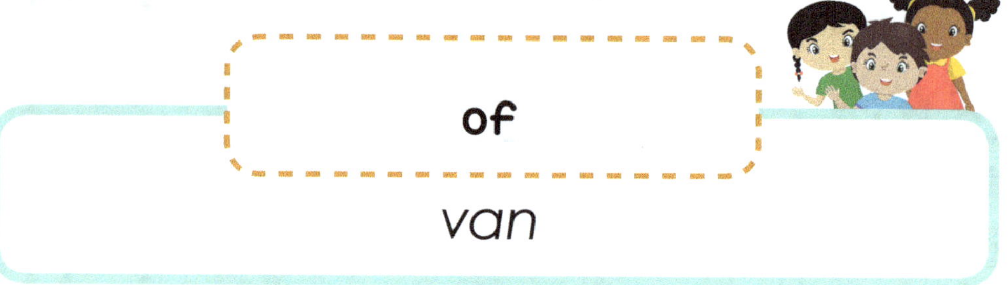

of
van

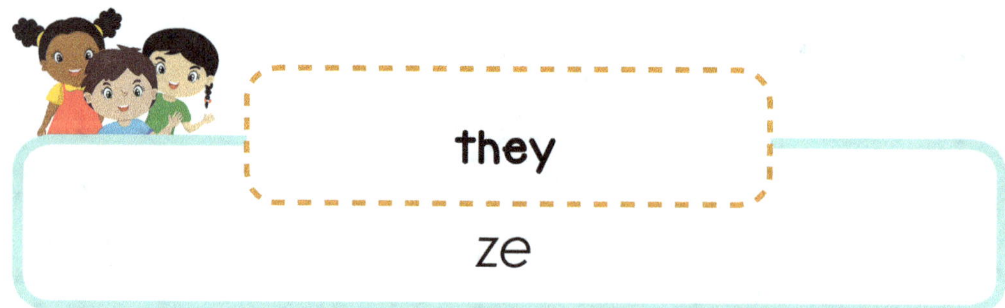

they
ze

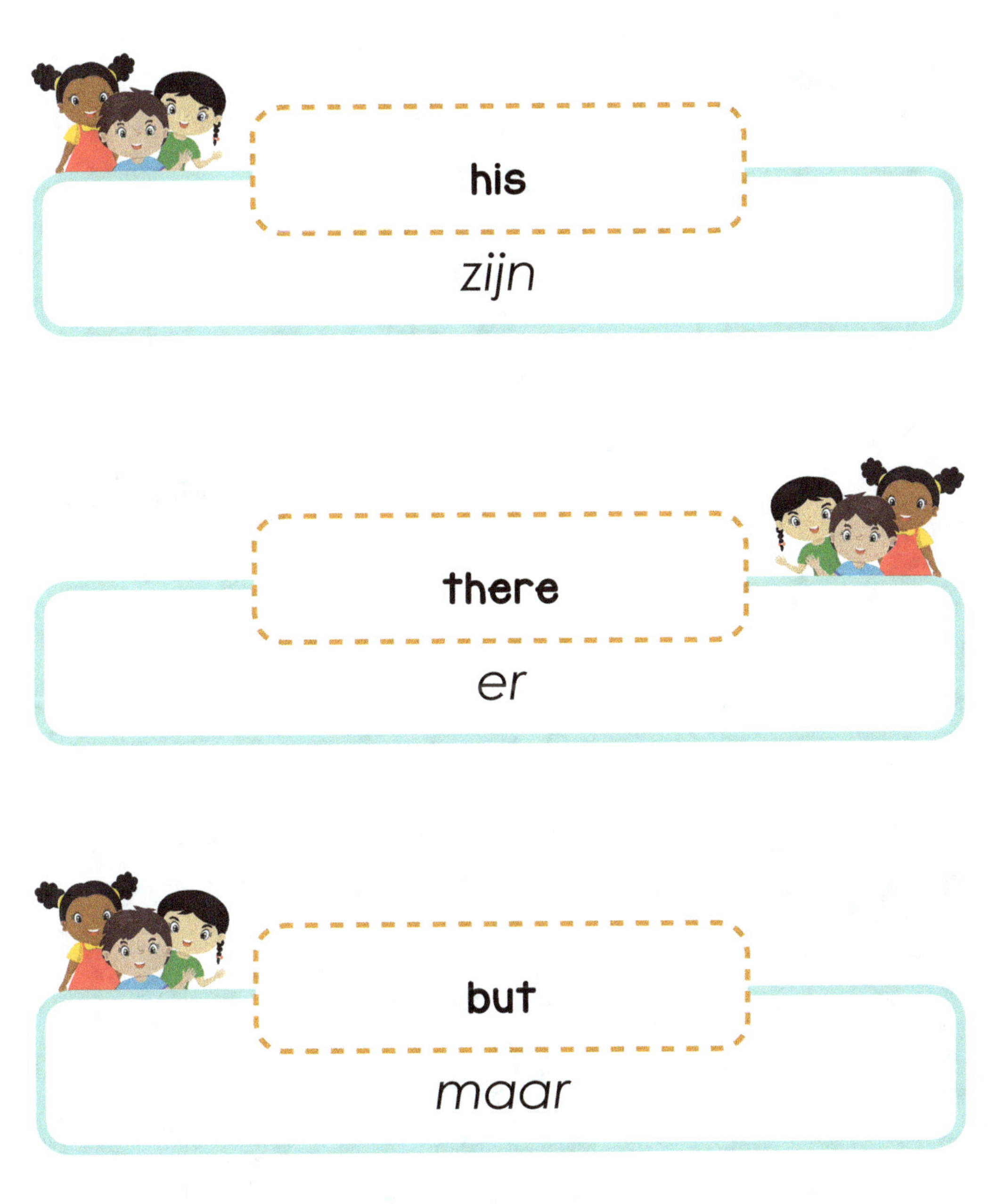

his
zijn
there
er
but
maar

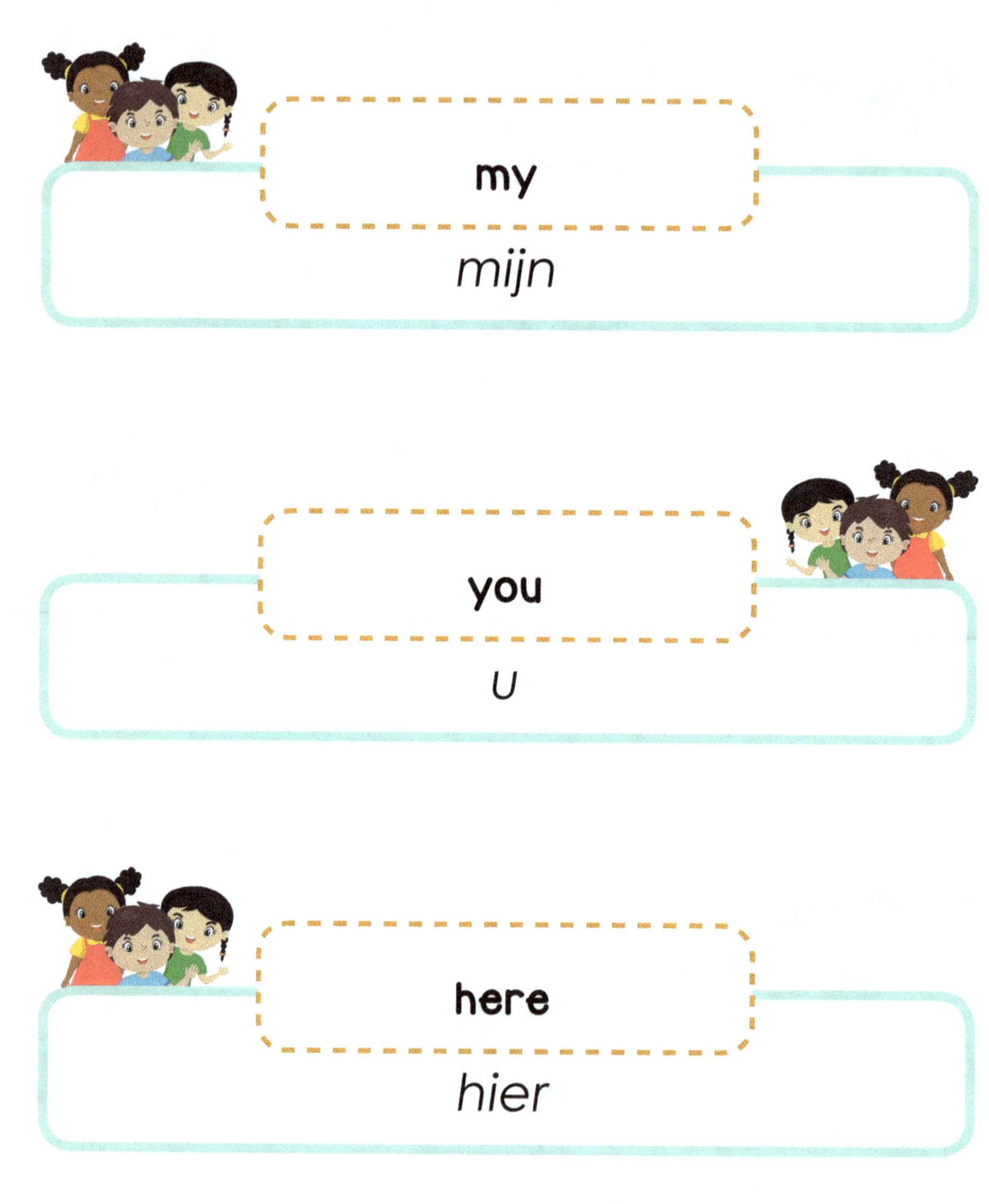

my

mijn

you

U

here

hier

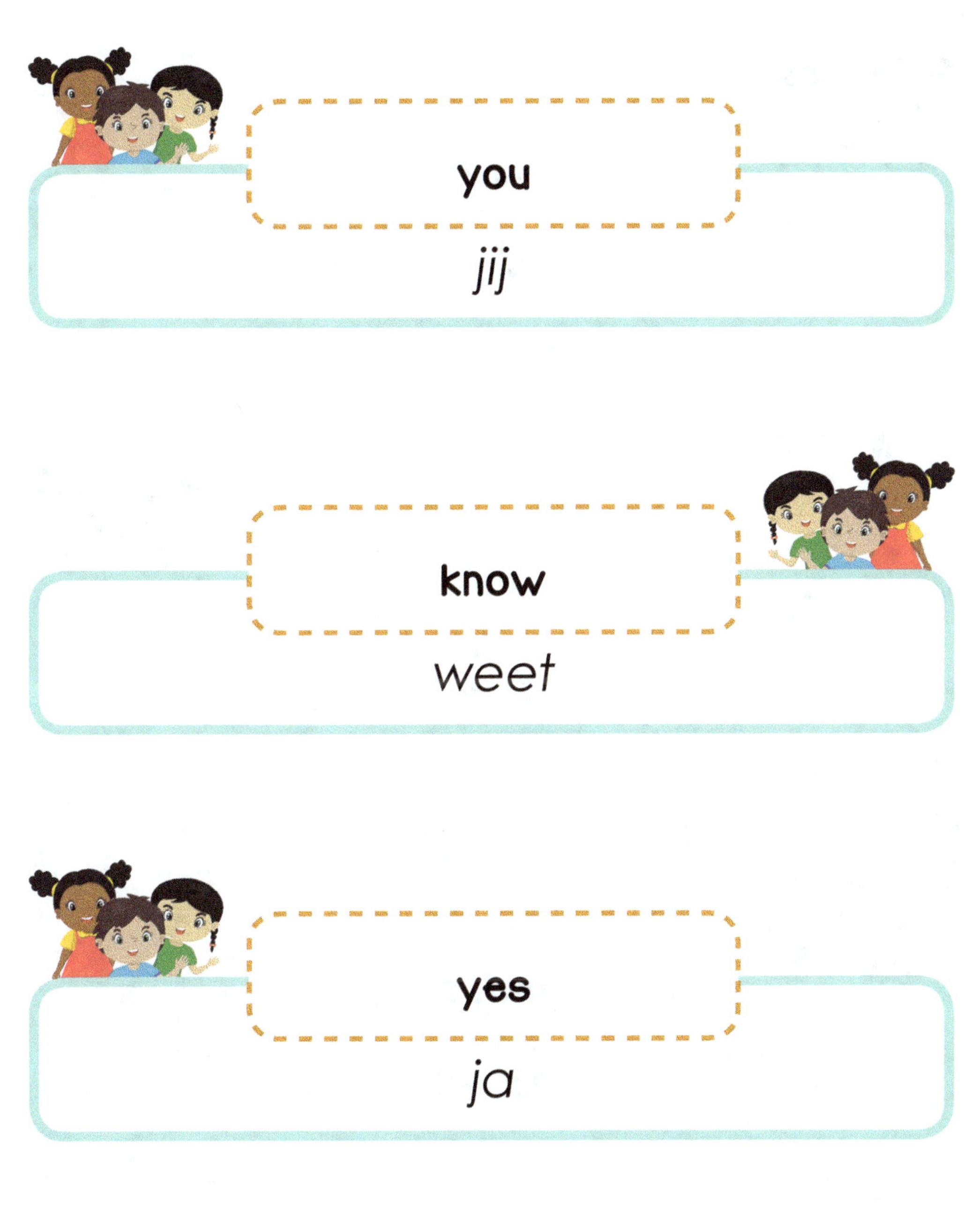

you
jij
know
weet
yes
ja

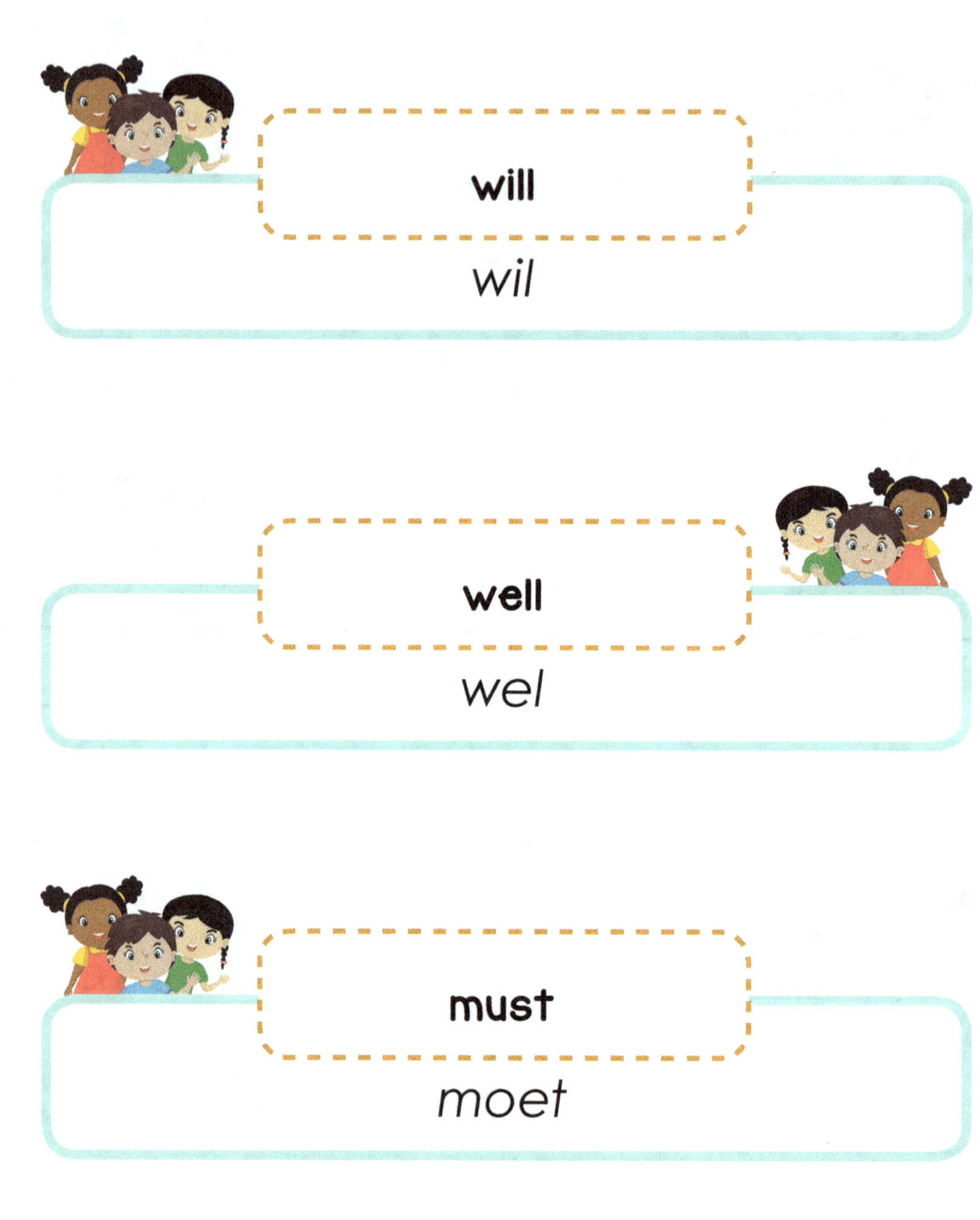

will
wil
well
wel
must
moet

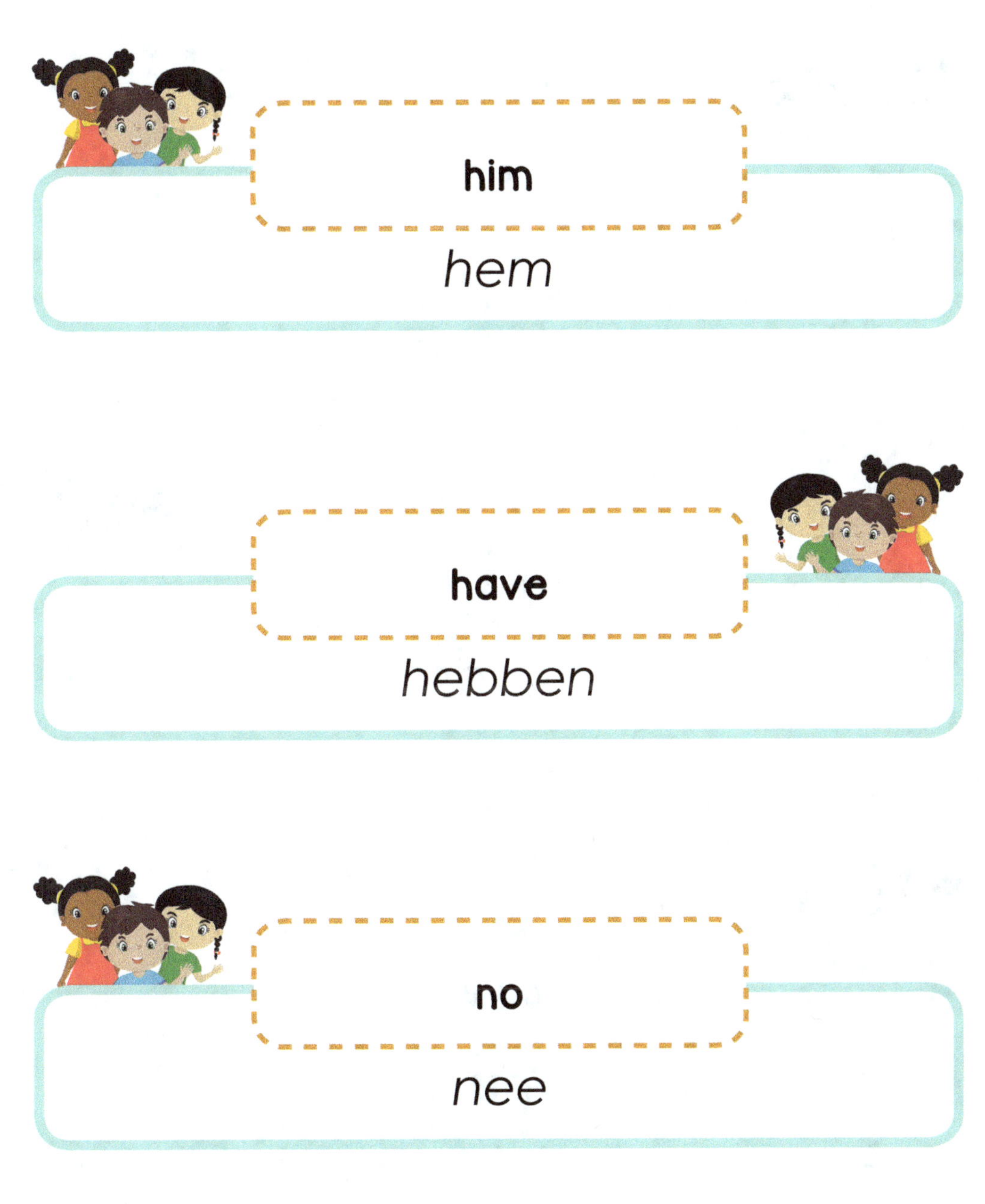

him
hem

have
hebben

no
nee

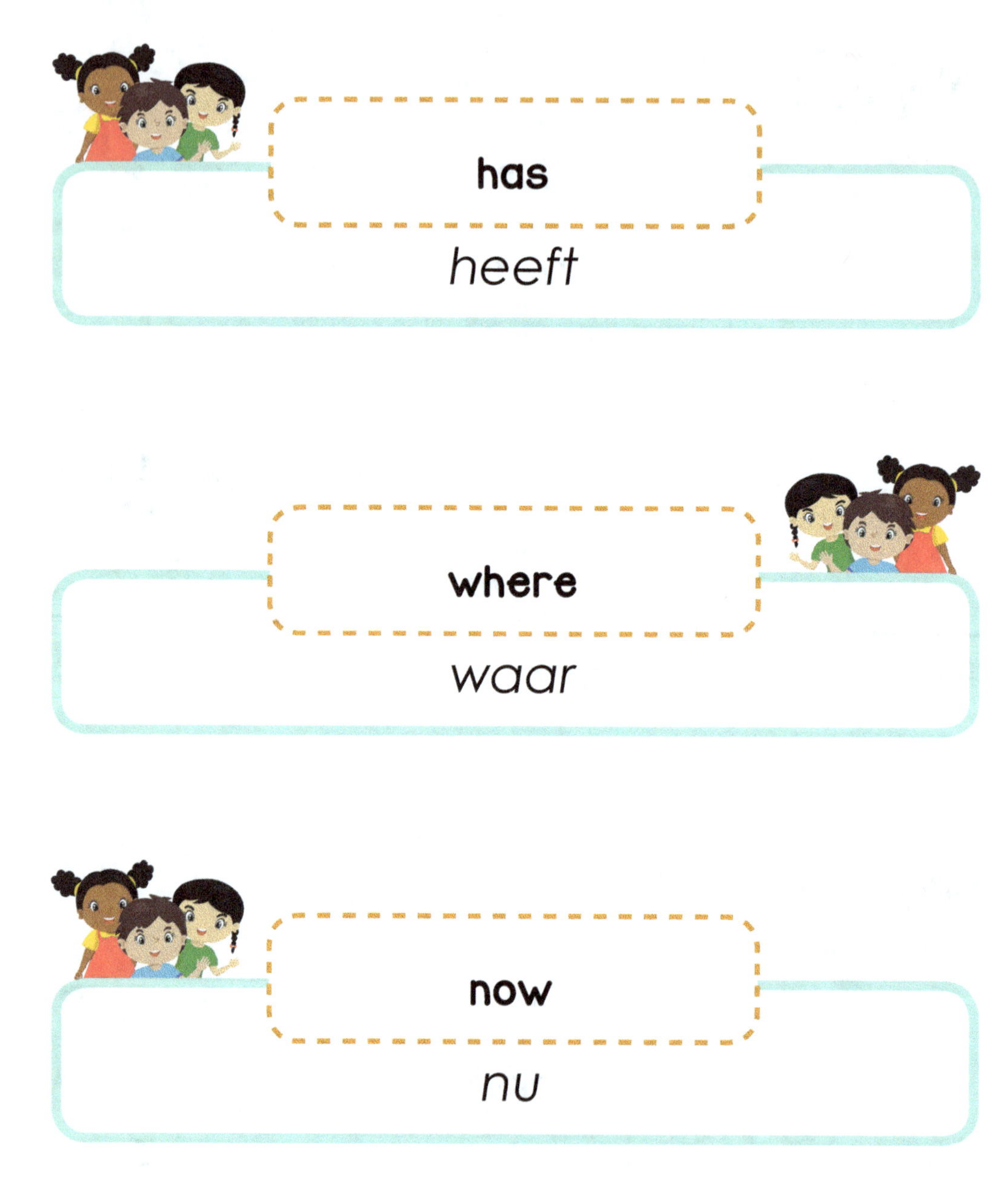

has
heeft
where
waar
now
nu

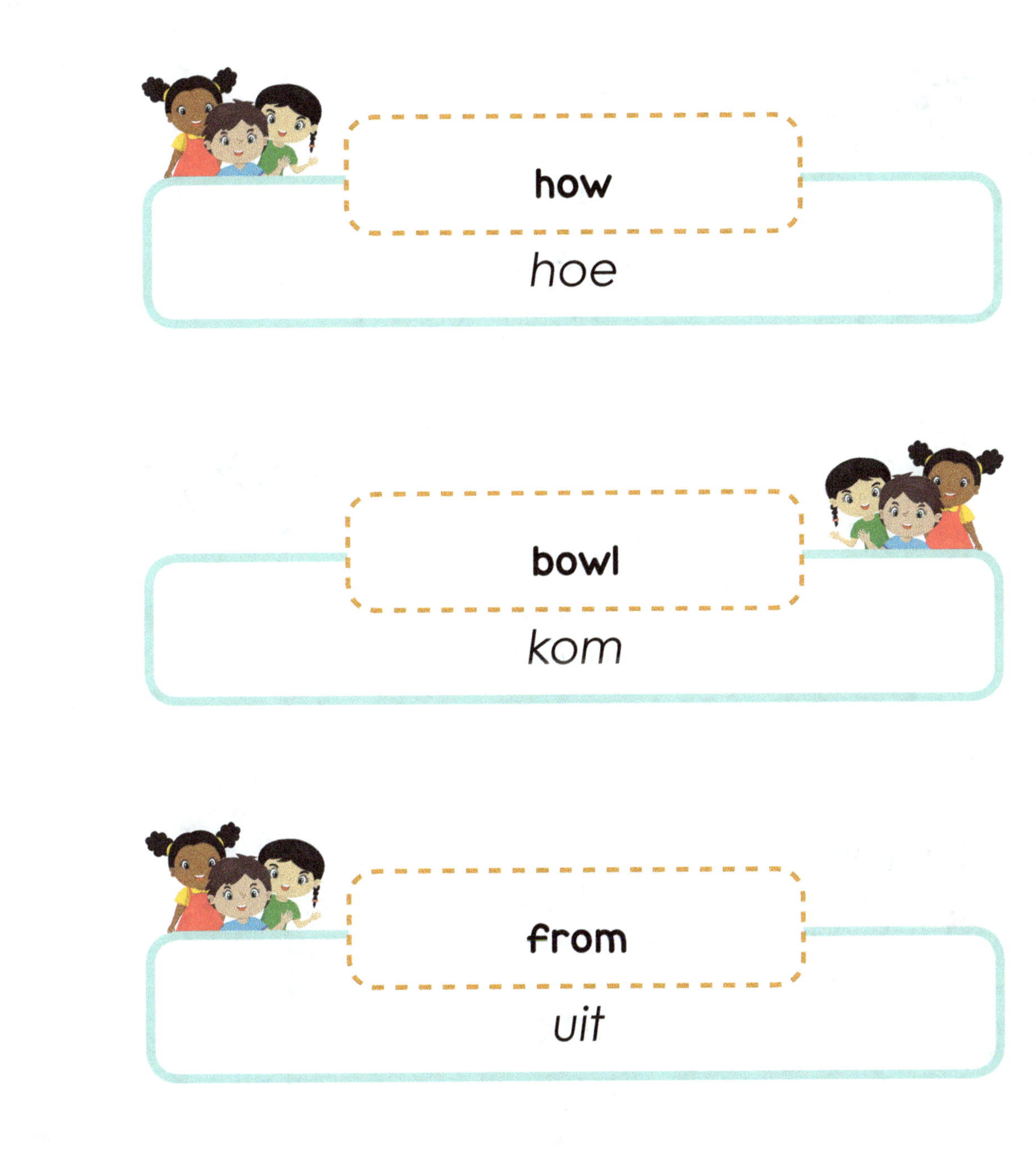
how
hoe
bowl
kom
from
uit

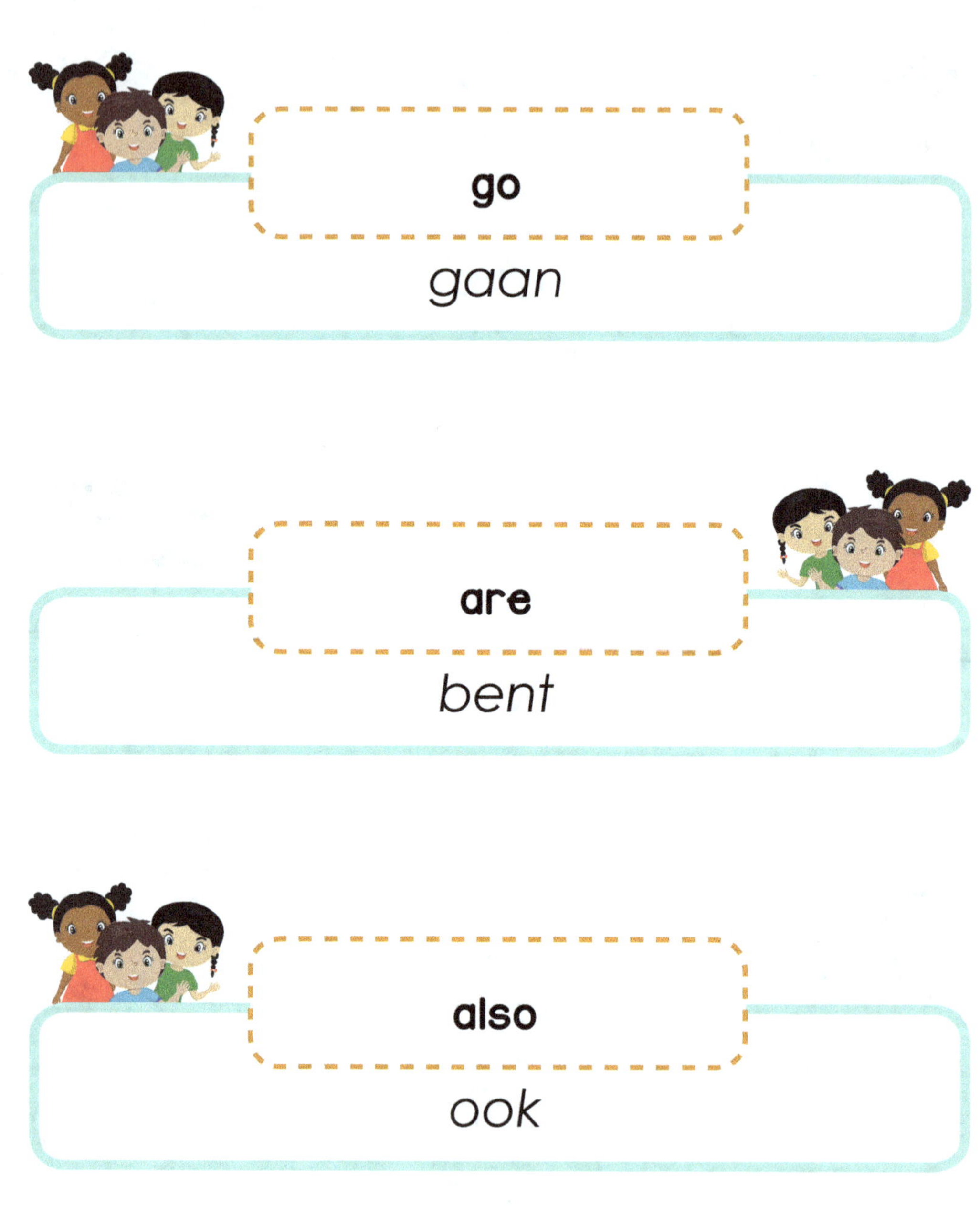

go
gaan

are
bent

also
ook

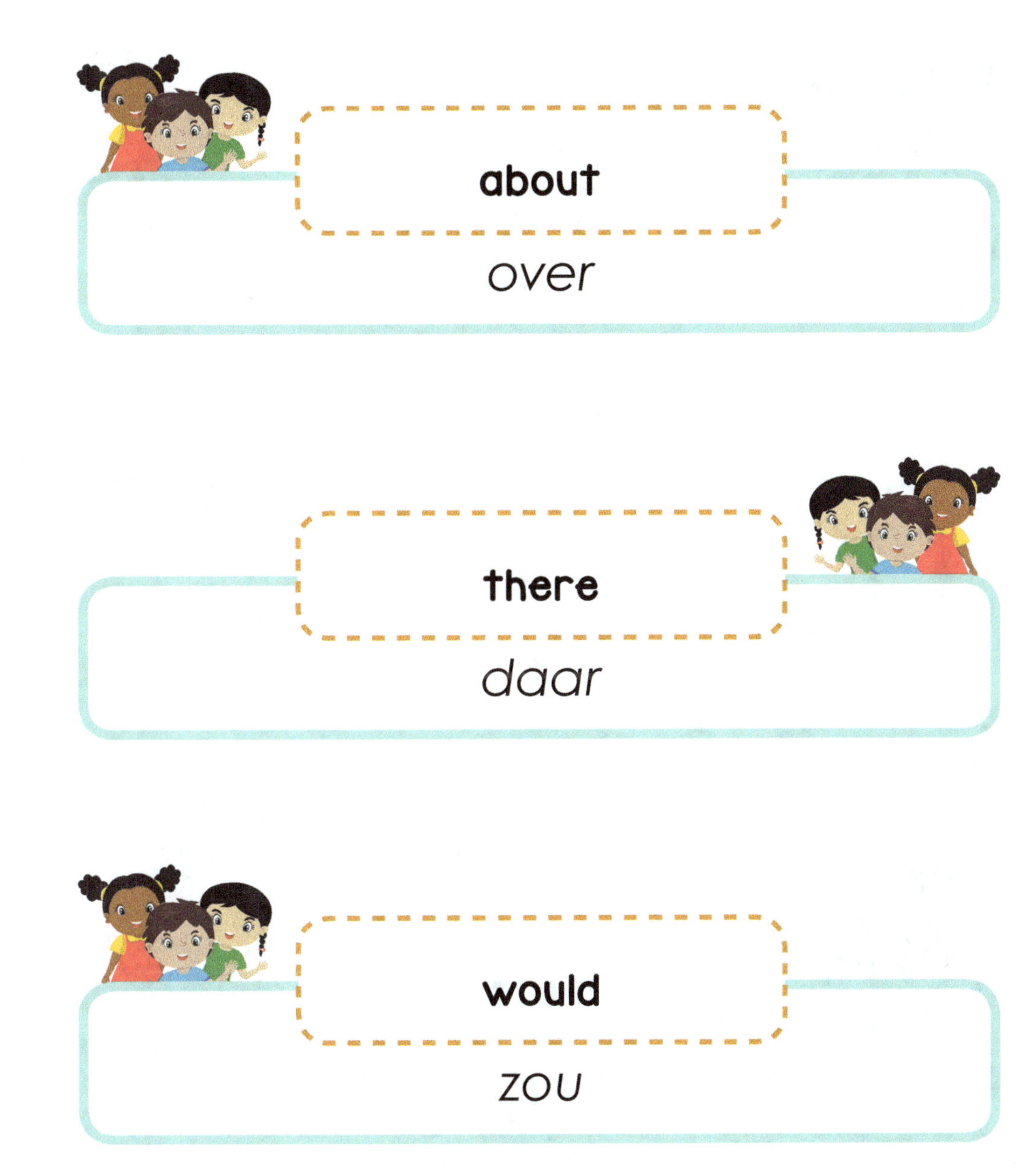

about
over

there
daar

would
zou

already
al
you
jullie
more
meer

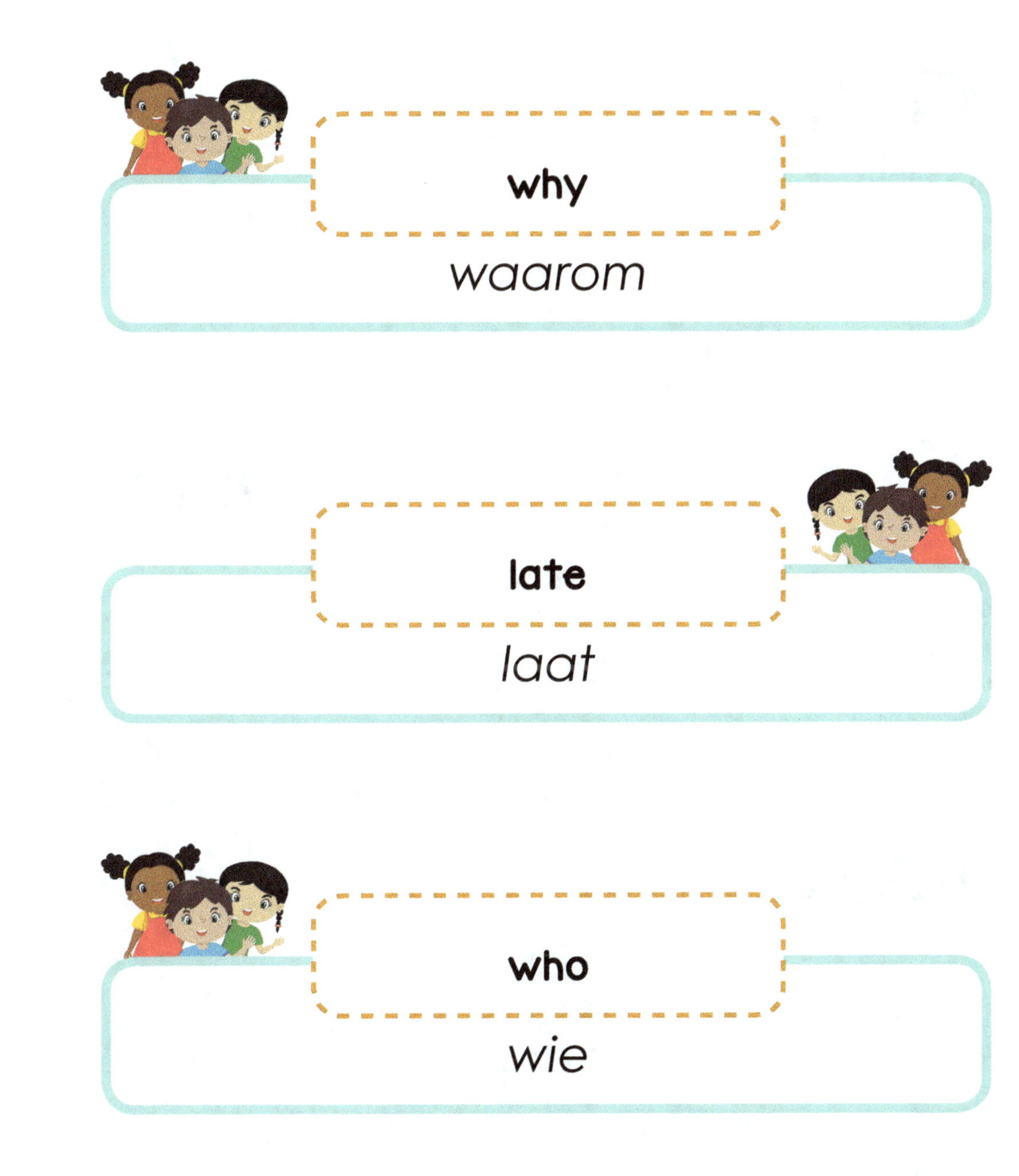

why
waarom
late
laat
who
wie

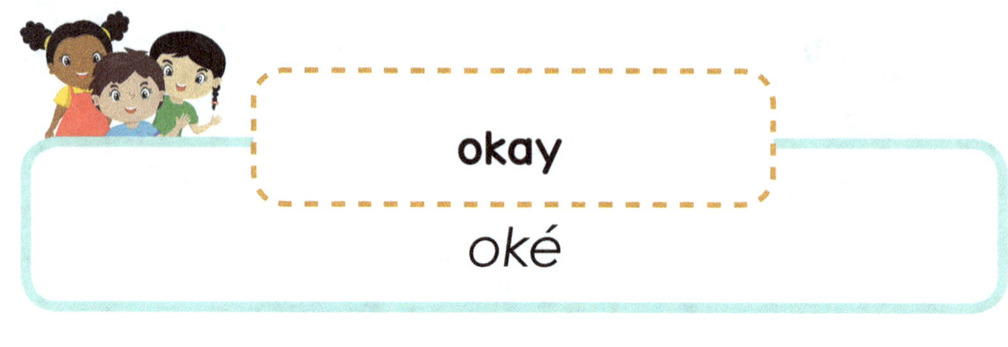

okay

oké

think

denk

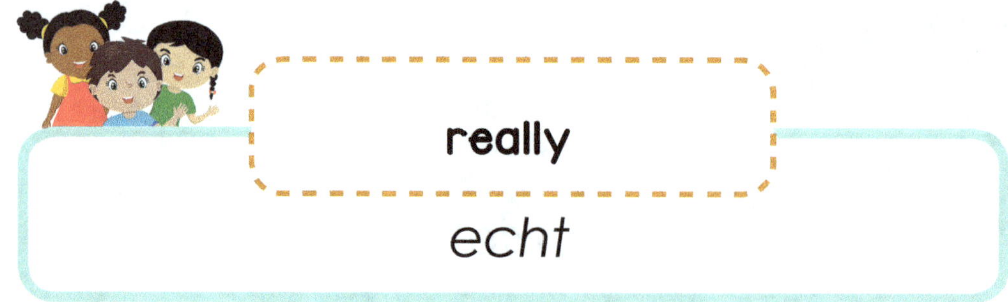

really

echt

MATCHING EXERCISE

Draw a line to match the English word to its Dutch word.

they	•		•	weet
know	•		•	wat
yes	•		•	nu
what	•		•	ze
have	•		•	daar
now	•		•	ja
there	•		•	wie
who	•		•	hebben

Now let's try
Dutch phrases.

English

Good Morning

Dutch

Goedemorgen

Pronunciation

khoo-duh-mawr-ghuh

English

Good Day

Dutch

Goedemiddag

Pronunciation

khoo-duh-mih-dahkh

Good Evening

Dutch

Goedenavond

Pronunciation

khoo-duh-nah-fohnt

English

Good Night

Dutch

Goedenacht

Pronunciation

khoo-duh-nahkht

Hi / Bye

Dutch

Hoi / Hallo / Daag / Doei

Pronunciation

hoy / hah-loh / dahk / doo-ee

English

Goodbye

Dutch

Tot ziens

Pronunciation

toht zeens

English
See you later

Dutch
Tot straks
Pronunciation
toht straks

English
See you soon

Dutch
Tot zo
Pronunciation
toht zoh

Thank you

Dutch

Dank u wel / Dank je wel

Pronunciation

dahnk-ew-vehl

Thank you very much

Dutch

Hartelijk bedankt

Pronunciation

hahr-tuh-lik buh-dahnkt

You're welcome

I'm sorry / Excuse me

Pardon me

How are you?

Fine / Very well

Dutch

Goed / Heel goed

Pronunciation

khoot / hayl khoot

English

I'm tired / sick.

Dutch

Ik ben moe / ziek

Pronunciation

ik ben moo / zeek

I'm hungry.

Ik heb honger

ik heb hohng-ur

What's your name?

Hoe heet u?

hoo hayt ew

My name is...

Dutch

Ik heet...

Pronunciation

ik hayt...

English

I am...

Dutch

Ik ben...

Pronunciation

ik ben

English

Nice to meet you.

Dutch

Aangenaam (kennis te maken)

Pronunciation

ahn-guh-nahm
(ken-nis tuh mah-kuh)

English

Where are you from?

Dutch

Waar komt u vandaan?

Pronunciation

vahr kawmt ew fun-dahn

English

I am from the Netherlands.

Dutch

Ik kom uit Nederland.

Pronunciation

ik kawm owt nay-der-lant

English

Where do you live?

Dutch

Waar woont u?

Pronunciation

vahr vohnt ew

How old are you?

Hoe oud bent u?

hoo owt bent ew

Do you speak Dutch?

Spreekt u Nederlands?

spraykt ew nay-der-lahnds

Have fun!

Dutch

Veel plezier!

Pronunciation

fayl pleh-zeer

Good luck!

Dutch

Veel succes!

Pronunciation

fayl suk-sehs

I love you.

Ik hou van je.

ik how fahn yuh

Be careful!

Wees voorzichtig!

vays fohr-zikh-tikh

Let's have
some fun with
Dutch words!

Fill in the blank with the correct Dutch word.

ENGLISH	DUTCH
today	vandaag

ENGLISH

today at 6:15

DUTCH

___________ om kwart over zes

ENGLISH	DUTCH
tomorrow	morgen

ENGLISH

tomorrow at 10:10

DUTCH

___________ om tien over tien

Fill in the blank with the correct Dutch word.

ENGLISH	DUTCH
yesterday	gisteren

ENGLISH

yesterday morning

DUTCH

______________ochtend

ENGLISH	DUTCH
calendar	kalender

ENGLISH

one calendar year

DUTCH

een ______________jaar

Fill in the blank with the correct Dutch word.

ENGLISH

second

DUTCH

seconde

ENGLISH

for one second

DUTCH

voor een ______________

ENGLISH

hour

DUTCH

uur

ENGLISH

for one hour

DUTCH

voor een ____________

Fill in the blank with the correct Dutch word.

ENGLISH

DUTCH

minute

minuut

ENGLISH

one minute

DUTCH

een ______________

ENGLISH

DUTCH

clock

klok

ENGLISH

wall clock

DUTCH

wand__________

Fill in the blank with the correct Dutch word.

ENGLISH	DUTCH
ugly	lelijk

ENGLISH

ugly face

DUTCH

_____________ gezicht

ENGLISH	DUTCH
beautiful	mooi

ENGLISH

beautiful actress

DUTCH

_____________e actrice

Fill in the blank with the correct Dutch word.

ENGLISH	DUTCH
good	goed

ENGLISH

good for one's body

DUTCH

____________ voor iemand zijn lichaam

ENGLISH	DUTCH
far	ver

ENGLISH

The woman is looking at something far away.

DUTCH

De vrouw kijkt naar iets ________ weg.

Fill in the blank with the correct Dutch word.

ENGLISH   **DUTCH**

see   zien

ENGLISH

see something

DUTCH

iets _________

ENGLISH   **DUTCH**

make   maken

ENGLISH

make coffee

DUTCH

koffle _________

Fill in the blank with the correct Dutch word.

ENGLISH	DUTCH
laugh	lachen

ENGLISH

laugh at something funny

DUTCH

____________ om iets grappigs

ENGLISH	DUTCH
come	komen

ENGLISH

come to mind

DUTCH

op een gedachte ____________

Fill in the blank with the correct Dutch word.

ENGLISH	DUTCH
go	gaan

ENGLISH

go fast

DUTCH

snel ___________

ENGLISH	DUTCH
do	doen

ENGLISH

to do it all

DUTCH

Alles ___________

Fill in the blank with the correct Dutch word.

ENGLISH   **DUTCH**

use   gebruiken

ENGLISH

use a webcam

DUTCH

webcam ____________

ENGLISH   **DUTCH**

can   kunnen

ENGLISH

can jump over

DUTCH

overheen ____________ springen

Fill in the blank with the correct Dutch word.

ENGLISH	DUTCH
difficult	moeilijk

ENGLISH

difficult job

DUTCH

______________ baan

ENGLISH	DUTCH
bad	slecht

ENGLISH

bad weather

DUTCH

______________ weer

Fill in the blank with the correct Dutch word.

ENGLISH	DUTCH
near	dichtbij

ENGLISH

near the city

DUTCH

_______________ de stad

ENGLISH	DUTCH
January	januari

ENGLISH

Tuesday, January 1st

DUTCH

dinsdag een (1) _______________

Fill in the blank with the correct Dutch word.

ENGLISH	DUTCH
February	februari

ENGLISH

February 29th

DUTCH

negenentwintig (29) _______________

ENGLISH	DUTCH
March	maart

ENGLISH

March 17th

DUTCH

zeventien (17) _______________

Fill in the blank with the correct Dutch word.

ENGLISH	DUTCH
April	april

ENGLISH

April first

DUTCH

een ___________

ENGLISH	DUTCH
June	juni

ENGLISH

June wedding

DUTCH

___________ trouwerij

Fill in the blank with the correct Dutch word.

ENGLISH	DUTCH
July	juli

ENGLISH

month of July

DUTCH

de maand ____________

ENGLISH	DUTCH
August	augustus

ENGLISH

hot August day

DUTCH

hete ____________ dag

Fill in the blank with the correct Dutch word.

ENGLISH	DUTCH
September	september

ENGLISH

September 1st

DUTCH

een ________________

ENGLISH	DUTCH
October	oktober

ENGLISH

on October 13th

DUTCH

op dertien (13) ______________

Fill in the blank with the correct Dutch word.

ENGLISH	DUTCH
November	november

ENGLISH

Thanksgiving, Thursday November 24th

DUTCH

Thanksgiving, donderdag vierentwintig (24) ___________________

ENGLISH	DUTCH
December	december

ENGLISH

December 25th

DUTCH

vijfentwintig (25) ______________

Fill in the blank with the correct Dutch word.

ENGLISH	DUTCH
zero	nul

ENGLISH

number zero

DUTCH

nummer __________

ENGLISH	DUTCH
one	een

ENGLISH

one degree

DUTCH

__________ graad

Fill in the blank with the correct Dutch word.

ENGLISH	DUTCH
two	twee

ENGLISH

two degrees

DUTCH

____________ graden

ENGLISH	DUTCH
three	drie

ENGLISH

number three

DUTCH

nummer  ____________

Fill in the blank with the correct Dutch word.

ENGLISH	DUTCH
four	vier

ENGLISH

four corners

DUTCH

___________ hoeken

ENGLISH	DUTCH
five	vijf

ENGLISH

five degrees

DUTCH

___________ graden

Fill in the blank with the correct Dutch word.

ENGLISH	DUTCH
six	zes

ENGLISH

six degrees

DUTCH

__________ graden

ENGLISH	DUTCH
seven	zeven

ENGLISH

seven things

DUTCH

__________ dingen

Fill in the blank with the correct Dutch word.

ENGLISH	DUTCH
eight	acht

ENGLISH

eight things

DUTCH

__________ dingen

ENGLISH	DUTCH
nine	negen

ENGLISH

nine degrees

DUTCH

__________ graden

Fill in the blank with the correct Dutch word.

ENGLISH **DUTCH**

ten tien

ENGLISH

ten degrees

DUTCH

_____________ graden

ENGLISH **DUTCH**

coffee koffie

ENGLISH

cup of coffee

DUTCH

kop _____________

Fill in the blank with the correct Dutch word.

ENGLISH	DUTCH
tea	thee

ENGLISH

drink tea

DUTCH

drink ___________

ENGLISH	DUTCH
wine	wijn

ENGLISH

glass of wine

DUTCH

glas ___________

ANSWER KEY

MATCHING EXERCISE

Draw a line to match the English word to its Dutch word.

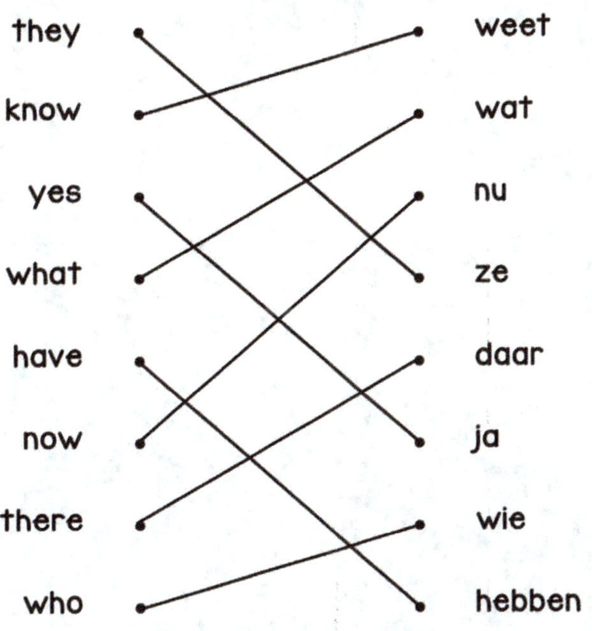

Visit
BABY PROFESSOR
EDUCATION KIDS
www.BabyProfessorBooks.com
to download Free Baby Professor eBooks
and view our catalog of new and exciting
Children's Books